CW00688614

by Iain Gray

LangSyne

PUBLISHING

WRITING *to* REMEMBER

Lang**Syne**

PUBLISHING

WRITING *to* REMEMBER

79 Main Street, Newtongrange,
Midlothian EH22 4NA
Tel: 0131 344 0414   Fax: 0845 075 6085
E-mail: info@lang-syne.co.uk
www.langsyneshop.co.uk

Design by Dorothy Meikle
Printed by Ricoh Print Scotland
© Lang Syne Publishers Ltd 2015

ISBN 978-1-85217-665-5

Parry

MOTTO:
Without God,
without anything,
God is enough.

CREST:
Three battle axes.

NAME variations include:
Parrey
Parrie
Perre

Chapter one:

Origins of Welsh surnames

by Iain Gray

If you don't know where you came from, you won't know where you're going is a frequently quoted observation and one that has a particular resonance today when there has been a marked upsurge in interest in genealogy, with increasing numbers of people curious to trace their family roots.

Main sources for genealogical research include census returns and official records of births, marriages and deaths – and the key to unlocking the detail they contain is obviously a family surname, one that has been 'inherited' and passed from generation to generation.

No matter our station in life, we all have a surname – but it was not until about the middle of the fourteenth century that the practice of being identified by a particular, or 'fixed', surname became commonly established throughout the British Isles.

Previous to this, it was normal for a person to be identified through the use of only a forename.

Wales, however, known in the Welsh language as *Cymru*, is uniquely different – with the use of what are known as patronymic names continuing well into the fifteenth century and, in remote rural areas, up until the early nineteenth century.

Patronymic names are ones where a son takes his father's forename, or Christian name, as his surname.

Examples of patronymic names throughout the British Isles include 'Johnson', indicating 'son of John', while specifically in Scotland 'son of' was denoted by the prefix Mc or Mac – with 'MacDonald', for example, meaning 'son of Donald.'

Early Welsh law, known as *Cyfraith Hywel*, *The Law of Hywel*, introduced by Hywel the Good, who ruled from Prestatyn to Pembroke between 915 AD and 950 AD, stipulated that a person's name should indicate their ancestry – the name in effect being a type of 'family tree.'

This required the prefixes *ap* or *ab* – derived from *mab*, meaning 'son of' being placed before the person's baptismal name.

In the case of females, the suffixes *verch* or *ferch*, sometimes shortened to *vch* or *vz* would be attached to their Christian name to indicate 'daughter of.'

In some cases, rather than being known for

example as *Llewellyn ap Thomas – Llewellyn son of Thomas* – Llewellyn's name would incorporate an 'ancestral tree' going back much earlier than his father.

One source gives the example of *Llewellyn ap Thomas ap Dafydd ap Evan ap Owen ap John* – meaning *Llewellyn son of Thomas son of Dafydd son of Evan son of Owen son of John.*

This leads to great confusion, to say the least, when trying to trace a person's ancestry back to a particular family – with many people having the forenames, for example, of Llewellyn, Thomas, Owen or John.

The first Act of Union between Wales and England that took place in 1536 during the reign of Henry VIII required that all Welsh names be registered in an Anglicised form – with *Hywel*, for example, becoming Howell, or Powell, and *Gruffydd* becoming Griffiths.

An early historical example of this concerns William ap John Thomas, standard bearer to Henry VIII, who became William Jones.

In many cases – as in Davies and Williams – an s was simply added to the original patronymic name, while in other cases the prefix *ap* or *ab* was contracted to *p* or *b* to prefix the name – as in *ab Evan* to form Bevan and *ap Richard* to form Pritchard.

Other original Welsh surnames – such as Morgan, originally *Morcant* – derive from ancient Celtic sources, while others stem from a person's physical characteristics – as in *Gwyn* or *Wynne* a nickname for someone with fair hair, *Gough* or *Gooch* denoting someone with red hair or a ruddy complexion, *Gethin* indicating swarthy or ugly and *Lloyd* someone with brown or grey hair.

With many popular surnames found today in Wales being based on popular Christian names such as John, this means that what is known as the 'stock' or 'pool' of names is comparatively small compared to that of common surnames found in England, Scotland and Ireland.

This explains why, in a typical Welsh village or town with many bearers of a particular name not necessarily being related, they were differentiated by being known, for example, as 'Jones the butcher', 'Jones the teacher' and 'Jones the grocer.'

Another common practice, dating from about the nineteenth century, was to differentiate among families of the same name by prefixing it with the mother's surname or hyphenating the name.

The history of the origins and development of Welsh surnames is inextricably bound up with the nation's frequently turbulent history and its rich culture.

Speaking a Celtic language known as Brythonic, which would gradually evolve into Welsh, the natives were subjected to Roman invasion in 48 AD, and in the following centuries to invasion by the Anglo-Saxons, Vikings and Normans.

Under England's ruthless and ambitious Edward I, the nation was fortified with castles between 1276 and 1295 to keep the 'rebellious' natives in check – but this did not prevent a series of bloody uprisings against English rule that included, most notably, Owain Glyndŵr's rebellion in 1400.

Politically united with England through the first Act of Union in 1536, becoming part of the Kingdom of Great Britain in 1707 and part of the United Kingdom in 1801, it was in 1999 that *Cynulliad Cenedlaethol Cymru*, the National Assembly for Wales, was officially opened by the Queen.

Welsh language and literature has flourished throughout the nation's long history.

In what is known as the Heroic Age, early Welsh poets include the late sixth century Taliesin and Aneirin, author of *Y Gododdin*.

Discovered in a thirteenth century manuscript but thought to date from anywhere between the seventh and eleventh centuries, it refers to the kingdom of Gododdin that took in south-east Scotland and

Northumberland and was part of what was once the Welsh territory known as *Hen Ogledd*, *The Old North*.

Commemorating Gododdin warriors who were killed in battle against the Angles of Bernicia and Deira at Catraith in about 600 AD, the manuscript – known as *Llyfr Aneirin*, *Book of Aneirin* – is now in the precious care of Cardiff City Library.

Other important early works by Welsh poets include the fourteenth century *Red Book of Hergest*, now held in the Bodleian Library, Oxford, and the *White Book of Rhydderch*, kept in the National Library of Wales, Aberystwyth.

William Morgan's translation of the Bible into Welsh in 1588 is hailed as having played an important role in the advancement of the Welsh language, while in 1885 Dan Isaac Davies founded the first Welsh language society.

It was in 1856 that Evan James and his son James James composed the rousing Welsh national anthem *Hen Wlad Fynhadad – Land of My Fathers*, while in the twentieth century the poet Dylan Thomas gained international fame and acclaim with poems such as *Under Milk Wood*.

The nation's proud cultural heritage is also celebrated through *Eisteddfod Genedlaethol Cymru*, the National Eisteddfod of Wales, the annual festival of music, literature and performance that is held across the nation and which traces its roots back to 1176 when Rhys ap Gruffyd, who ruled the territory of Deheubarth from 1155 to 1197, hosted a magnificent festival of poetry and song at his court in Cardigan.

The 2011 census for Wales unfortunately shows that the number of people able to speak the language has declined from 20.8% of the population of just under 3.1 million in 2001 to 19% – but overall the nation's proud culture, reflected in its surnames, still flourishes.

Many Welsh families proudly boast the heraldic device known as a Coat of Arms, as featured on our front cover.

The central motif of the Coat of Arms would originally have been what was borne on the shield of a warrior to distinguish himself from others on the battlefield.

Not featured on the Coat of Arms, but highlighted on page three, is the family motto and related crest – with the latter frequently different from the central motif.

Echoes of a far distant past can still be found in our surnames and they can be borne with pride in commemoration of our forebears.

Chapter two:

Intrigue and conspiracy

Derived from the popular forename 'Harry', in turn a pet form, or diminutive of 'Henry', 'Parry' is a patronymic surname of uniquely Welsh roots indicating 'son of Harry', while 'Henry' – of Germanic origin – denotes 'head, or chief, of the household.'

The Welsh form of the surname is 'ap Harry' – 'son of Harry' – and 'Parry' was formed through contracting 'ap' to 'p' and prefixing it to 'Harry' after dropping the 'h'.

The name is of ancient provenance and is particularly identified with Caernarfonshire, one of the thirteen historic Welsh counties.

Also known as Caernarvonshire and Carnarvonshire and in Welsh as *Sir Gaernarfon* – with 'Sir' denoting 'County' – it was once part of the former kingdom of Gwynedd.

In common with other ancient Welsh kingdoms, it fell victim to the Normans following their Conquest of England in October of 1066.

Duke William II of Normandy was declared King of England on December 25, and the complete subjugation of his Anglo-Saxon subjects followed, with those Normans who had fought on his behalf rewarded with lands – a pattern that would be followed in Wales.

Invading across the Welsh Marches, the borderland between England and Wales, the Normans gradually consolidated their gains.

But, under a succession of Welsh leaders who included Llywelyn ap Gruffudd, known as Llywelyn the Last, resistance proved strong.

But Llwelyn's resistance was brutally crushed in 1283 under England's ruthless and ambitious Edward I, who ordered the building or repair of at least 17 castles and in 1302 proclaimed his son and heir, the future Edward II, as Prince of Wales, a title known in Welsh as *Tywysog Cymru*.

Another heroic Welsh figure dominated the resistance movement from 1400 to 1415 in the form of Owain Glyndŵr – the last native Welshman to be recognised by his supporters as *Tywysog Cymru*.

In what is known as The Welsh Revolt he achieved an early series of stunning victories against Henry IV and his successor Henry V – until mysteriously disappearing from the historical record after mounting an ambush in Brecon.

Some sources assert that he was either killed in the ambush or died a short time afterwards from wounds he received – but there is a persistent tradition that he survived and lived thereafter in anonymity, protected by loyal followers.

During the revolt, he had consistently refused offers of a Royal Pardon and – despite offers of hefty rewards for his capture – he was never betrayed.

Bearers of the Parry name feature prominently in the frequently turbulent drama that is the historical record – with a number having been closely involved in the life, times and royal court of Elizabeth I, who reigned from 1558 to 1603.

Born in about 1508 at Newcourt, Bacton, in the Dore Valley, Ewias, Herefordshire, Blanche Parry – whose surname is also sometimes rendered 'ap Harry' – served as a 'gentlewoman' to Elizabeth from the time she had been a three-year-old princess.

With powerful connections to the nobility, her family shared kinship with not only the earls of Pembroke but also the Cecil family – one of whose sons, William Cecil, Lord Burghley, served as the queen's Chief Minister.

By 1558, Blanche Parry is described as 'second gentlewoman' to the queen, while by 1565 she is ranked as 'first gentlewoman.'

Having known Elizabeth from an early age, she became one of her most trusted friends and confidantes – to the extent that some sources assert she served as 'mother figure', with the queen's mother having been the ill-fated Ann Boleyn, second wife of Henry VIII.

Her closeness to the queen made her an influential figure, able to recommend those deserving of patronage, while she herself was in receipt of what one source describes as "grateful legacies from persons aided by her."

Unmarried, she died in 1590 and was buried in St Margaret's Westminster, while she left a number of charitable bequests and legacies.

One of the most influential of the queen's advisors was the Welsh courtier Sir Thomas Parry.

His date of birth is not known, but he was born in Brecknockshire and, in common with Blanche Parry, shared a kinship with the Cecils.

Knighted by Elizabeth in 1558 as 'Thomas Parry of Wales' and in 1559 appointed Master of the Wards, he died a year later and was buried in Westminster Abbey.

His son, also named Sir Thomas Parry, knighted in 1605 by Elizabeth's successor James I (James VI of Scotland), served as ambassador to Paris, while in 1607 he was made a Privy Councillor.

His date of birth is not known, but he died in 1616 and, in common with his father, was buried in Westminster Abbey.

One particularly complex character who bore the Parry name was the Welsh courtier, spy and would-be royal assassin William Parry.

His date of birth is not known, but he was born in Northrop, Flintshire, the son of Harry ap David – described as a "gentleman" in contemporary sources and who had served in the royal guard.

When he died in 1566 he had fathered no less than an astonishing thirty children – fourteen by his first wife and sixteen by his second, William Parry's mother.

Originally known as William ap Harry, the ambitious and smooth-talking William Parry left his native Wales as a youth to seek fame and fortune in London.

Marriage to a widow brought him a comfortable income, and this was supplemented when he entered the household of William Herbert, 1st Earl of Pembroke.

Following the earl's death in 1570, Parry entered into Elizabeth's service but, despite his apparent wealth and, following the death of his first wife having married another lady of means, he fell heavily into debt.

To escape the creditors clamouring at his door, he sought a commission from Lord Burghley to spy on his behalf on Catholics on the Continent who were allegedly plotting the overthrow of the staunchly Protestant Elizabeth.

It is not known when he left for the Continent, but in 1577 he was back in England and, two years later, made another hasty exit to escape his ever-growing band of creditors.

For reasons that remain unclear, it was on this second sojourn to the Continent that he secretly converted to the Catholic faith, returning home a year later to find his creditors had finally raised court action against him.

Parry's response was to 'violently assault' one of them, a Hugh Hare – and the assault must indeed have been violent because he was convicted and sentenced to death.

Again for reasons that remain unclear, although it may have been through the influence of Elizabeth's trusted advisor Lord Burghley, the queen granted him a pardon, while he found surety for his debts through Sir John Conway, a relative on his mother's side of the family.

A possible reason why Burghley may have secured the pardon is that he was actually employing Parry as a 'double agent' – because in 1582 he was back on the Continent not only passing himself off as a Catholic supporter but also claiming he was intent on no less than the queen's assassination.

Apparently seeking approval for an assassination scheme from Catholic quarters in Italy and France, he returned to England in 1584 and voluntarily disclosed this to the queen – declaring that he was an *agent provocateur*, engaged in an elaborate game of deception to 'draw out' Catholic plotters and to cover Protestant plots.

He was believed and Elizabeth not only granted him a pension but also rewarded him with a Parliamentary seat.

Matters now become decidedly murky.

Yet again heavily in debt, he hoped to be financially rewarded by 'uncovering' a plot to assassinate the queen.

He accordingly approached the influential courtier Sir Edmund Neville – suspected of being a Catholic sympathiser – and suggested that the two of them should kill the queen during a private audience or while she was riding in her coach.

But Neville informed against him and Parry was seized and confined in the Tower of London on a charge of high treason.

His trial began in February of 1585 and, perhaps hoping for a pardon, plead guilty – but he later withdrew this, stating that his confession was "a tissue of falsehoods."

He was nevertheless condemned to death and hanged in Westminster Palace Yard in March of 1585 – declaring his innocence to the last.

Following his execution a government-approved tract, *A true and plaine Declaration of the Horrible Treasons practised by William Parry* was published – but to this day the jury still remains very much out as to whether or not the debt-ridden William Parry had indeed seriously plotted the queen's assassination.

Chapter three:

Scholastic renown

One colourful bearer of the Parry name was the Welsh scholar David Parry, born in about 1683 in Cardigan.

The son of William Parry, described by a contemporary source as "a poor man", he nevertheless managed to obtain an education at Cardigan Grammar School, where he excelled in Latin.

It was perhaps because of his academic prowess that he came to the attention of the Welsh geographer, linguist, antiquarian and botanist Edward Lhuyd – Keeper of the Ashmolean Museum in Oxford – who took him on his travels throughout Wales, Scotland and Brittany.

Arrested for a time in the latter country as spies, they returned to England in 1701, with Parry graduating three years later from Jesus College, Oxford.

Employed by Lhuyd as under-keeper at the Ashmolean, when Lhuyd died in 1709 Parry was appointed Keeper.

This was an unsalaried post, and it remains somewhat of a historical mystery how he managed to support himself.

Although considered very able, he acquired a reputation for having a particularly unfortunate relationship with alcohol.

One contemporary stated that he was "capable" if only "he could spare time from his pots and companions; but out of the tippling house he cannot spare one minute even to common civility."

Another source states how Parry, who died in 1714, "being a perfect sot he shortened his days, being just turned of thirty."

Born in 1786 in Llangar, Denbighshire, the son of a church rector, John Humffreys Parry was the Welsh barrister and antiquarian who met a particularly violent end.

Working for a time in the office of an uncle who was a solicitor, he went on to study law in London and was called to the bar in 1811.

After practising for a time as a solicitor and having inherited property when his father died, he abandoned his legal career in favour of antiquarian studies and writing.

Starting the *Cambro-Briton* publication on Welsh history in 1819, he was also involved in the re-establishment of the Cymmrodorian Society – the Welsh learned society first founded in 1750 but which had fallen into abeyance.

Winner of prizes in 1823 at the Carmarthen Eisteddfod for the two essays *The Ancient Manners and Customs of the Britons* and *The Navigation of the Britons*, he was attacked and killed in 1825 by a bricklayer with whom he had quarrelled in a tavern in Pentonville, London.

His son, also named John Humffreys Parry, was the barrister born in London in 1816.

Called to the bar in 1843, he was appointed a serjeant-at-law – a barrister of superior rank – in 1856.

In this capacity he was involved in a number of high profile cases, one of the most famous, where he had the responsibility for the indictment, that of The Tichborne Claimant a lengthy case at the time that involved both a civil trial and a criminal trial.

It concerned a curious claim by Thomas Castro, also known as Arthur Orton, that he was the missing heir to the Tichborne Baronetcy in Hampshire.

The heir to the family title and fortune was Roger Tichborne, who was believed to have died in a shipwreck in 1854 while returning from South America.

But his grieving mother, having heard rumours that he was alive and living in Australia, placed advertisements in newspapers throughout the length and breadth of Australia offering a reward for any information on her son.

In 1866 a butcher known as Thomas Castro and who had been living in Wagga Wagga, New South Wales, came forward with the claim that he was actually Roger Tichborne.

Although Lady Tichborne accepted his claim, the rest of the family were highly sceptical and raised a civil court action against him.

Extensive inquiries into his background were undertaken and the case did not come to law until 1871.

It then emerged that he might in fact be called Arthur Orton, a butcher's son from Wapping who had left home as a youth and had last been heard of in Australia.

His claim was dismissed and, charged with perjury, was later brought before a criminal court. Found guilty, he was sentenced to14 years imprisonment.

Later confessing that he was indeed Arthur Orton – only to immediately retract this – he died destitute in 1898.

Parry, meanwhile, a supporter of the Chartist movement that sought social justice and political equality and one of the founders of the Complete Suffrage Association, died in 1880.

In the twentieth century, Thomas Parry, later more formally known as Sir Thomas Parry, was the distinguished Welsh scholar and poet born in 1904 at

Brynawel, Carmel, in the early Parry heartland of Caernarfonshire.

The son of a quarryman and smallholder, he won a scholarship to University College of North Wales, Bangor in 1922 and, a year later, won the prestigious Crown at the Inter-collegiate Eisteddfod for his literary compositions and, a year after that, both the Crown and the Chair.

Some of his works were also published in 1924 in *Barddoniaeth Bangor*, while he graduated from university in 1926 with a first class honours degree in Welsh.

A number of academic posts subsequently followed, the first being an assistant lectureship in Welsh and Latin at the University College of South Wales and Monmouthshire, Cardiff.

In addition to publishing a number of works that include translations and song lyrics, his most noted work is his monumental study and edit of the works of the fourteenth century Welsh poet Dafydd ap Gwilym.

Beginning the work in 1929, it was finally published in 1954 and the *Dictionary of Welsh Biography* notes how: "It was immediately recognised as one of the masterpieces of Welsh scholarship."

Serving as Librarian of the National Library in Aberystwyth from 1953 to 1958 and elected a Fellow of the Royal Academy in 1959, he served until his retirement in 1969 as principal of the University College of Wales, Aberystwyth.

Also having held for a time the office of president of the National Library and chairman of the literature committee of the *New Welsh Bible*, he died in 1985, three years before the Bible was published.

Chapter four:

On the world stage

A noted eighteenth century Welsh portrait painter, William Parry was born in 1743.

In common with many other artists and musicians of the time, he relied on the support of wealthy patrons to advance his talent, and he was fortunate that his patron was Sir Watkin Williams-Wynn, 3rd Baronet of Wynnstay, in Denbighshire and recognised as the wealthiest Welshman of his day.

His father John Parry was a harpist in the baronet's household and it was through this connection that he came to his attention.

Born in the Llŷn Peninsula in what is now Gwynedd in about 1710, his father had been blind from birth and was known in Welsh as *Parri Ddall Rhiwason – Blind Parry of Ruabon –* and was famed as an expert on the Welsh triple harp.

An art lover, meanwhile, the baronet recognised William Parry's talents from an early age and arranged for him when he was aged sixteen to study at a drawing academy, while he was also able to become a pupil of the great English painter Joshua Reynolds.

Through the baronet's connections, Parry

received commissions for portraits of wealthy members of the Welsh gentry, while from 1770 to 1775 he undertook the Grand Tour of Europe.

Elected an associate of the Royal Academy in 1776 – having executed his most famous work, *Portrait of Omai with Sir Joseph Banks and Dr Daniel Solander* – he settled in Italy in 1789 following the death of his wife.

The reason for moving to Italy, according to one of his biographers, was "to seek employment in art, in addition to the wish of stifling the loss of an amiable wife."

But ill-health forced him to return to London, where he died in 1791.

Many of his works, including portraits of his father, are now in the care of the National Museum, Cardiff.

Born in 1816 in Banstead, Surrey, **Thomas Gambier Parry** was the English artist and art collector noted in artistic circles for having developed the Gambier Parry technique of fresco painting.

It was after studying the fresco technique of Italian painters that he developed his own process, executing mural projects in the parish church at Highnam, Gloucestershire – where he lived at Highnam Court – and in Ely Cathedral.

Having inherited his wealth from his grandfather and father who had been directors of the East India Company, he used it to not only accrue his impressive art collection but also for a number of philanthropic works that included the founding of a college of art and science, an orphanage and a children's hospital in Gloucester.

He also funded the building of the Church of the Holy Innocent, Highnam, and it was here that he was laid to rest after his death in 1888 in a tomb designed by his son Sidney.

His valuable art collection, which included the magnificent *Coronation of the Virgin* by the Italian artist Lorenzo Monaco, was bequeathed by his heirs to the Courtauld Institute, London and where some are displayed in the Courtauld Gallery.

He was the father of the composer **Sir Charles Parry**, renowned for works that include his 1916 *Jerusalem* – the music set for the William Blake poem of the name.

Born in 1848, created a baronet in 1902, professor of music at Oxford University from 1900 to 1908 and author of a number of works on music and music history, he died in 1918.

Noted as the composer of *Aberystwyth*, the hymn tune used in the South African national anthem

Nkosi Sikelel' iAfrika, **Joseph Parry** was born in Merthyr Tydfil in 1841 and immigrated to the United States with his family when he was aged 13.

Settling in Danville, Pennsylvania where there was an established community of fellow Welsh expatriates, he worked in an iron mill but also immersed himself in cultural activities such as the local eisteddfod – later adopting the bardic name *Pencerdd America*.

Admitted a Freemason in 1867, he later composed *Ysgytwad y Llaw – The Handshake –* in celebration of the Craft, while after returning to Britain he studied music at Cambridge University.

Appointed professor of music at the University of Wales in 1873, his 1876 opera *Blodwen* was performed worldwide, while his *Saul of Tarsus* oratorio was originally composed for the National Eisteddfod of 1892.

Also the composer of *Myfanwy* and the oratorio *Emmanuel*, he died in 1903 and was buried in Augustine's Churchyard, Penarth, Vale of Glamorgan.

In contemporary music, Richard Parry, better known as **Dick Parry**, is the English saxophonist who, as a session musician, has played on studio recordings for a number of bands – particularly Pink Floyd.

Born in 1942 in Kentford, Sussex he *contributed the solo saxophone part for the band's Us and Them, Shine On You Crazy Diamond* and *Money*, while he has also toured with them.

Bearers of the Parry name have also excelled in the highly competitive world of sport.

On the golf course, **John Parry** is the English professional player born in Harrogate in 1986.

Winner of a number of amateur tournaments including the Spanish and Danish Amateur Championships and having represented Great Britain and Northern Ireland in the Walker Cup before turning professional in 2007, major wins since include the 2009 Allianz Golf Open Toulouse in the Challenge Tour.

On the cricket pitch, **Stephen Parry**, born in Manchester in 1986 and nicknamed "Pazza", is the left-arm bowler and right-hand batsman who has played for England and clubs that include Lancashire and Cumberland.

On the football pitch, **Maurice Parry** was the talented Welsh international player born in 1877 in Trefonen, Oswestry.

Best known for having played 222 games for Liverpool, making his debut with the club in 1900 and over the next nine years helping them to win two Football League Championships, he also played for clubs that include Scottish team Partick Thistle.

He died in 1935, while his son **Frank Parry**,

born in Liverpool in 1898 and who died in 1973, earned 14 caps playing for Wales in addition to playing for clubs that include Everton, Grimbsy Town and Accrington Stanley; his uncle, **Thomas Parry**, also earned caps for his nation.

From sport to film **Richard Parry**, born in Kenya in 1967, is the director and cinematographer whose screen credits include the 2001 *A Night in the Woods* and, from 2008, *Blood Trail*.

Bearers of the proud name of Parry have also proven to be particularly intrepid adventurers and explorers.

Born in Bath in 1790, **Sir William Parry** was the Royal Navy rear-admiral and Arctic explorer who, in 1827, attempted one of the first expeditions to the North Pole.

Although unsuccessful, he and his team set the record for 'furthest north' – one that was not beaten until nearly fifty years later by Albert Hastings Markham.

Also leader of an expedition from 1818 to 1820 to find the elusive Northwest Passage – a sea route through the Arctic Ocean along the northern coast of North America and through the Canadian Arctic Archipelago to connect the Atlantic and Pacific oceans – he had to finally abandon the quest, although it appears to have been tantalisingly within his reach.

Recognised as having pioneered the use of canning techniques to preserve food while on his Arctic expeditions and knighted in 1829, he died in 1855, while places named in his honour include Parry Sound, Ontario and the crater Parry on the Moon.

Born in Gloucestershire in 1823 and settling in the United States with his parents when he was aged nine, **Charles Parry** was the eminent British-American botanist and mountaineer who discovered many species of new plants.

Having studied both botany and medicine at Columbia University, he was employed from 1848 to 1855 as a botanist and surgeon with the United States and Mexican Boundary Survey.

He collected valuable specimens while employed in this capacity, later extending his expeditions to Colorado and Utah.

Plants he discovered include the Torrey Pine and the Engelmann Spruce – named by him in honour of two of his teachers and mentors at Columbia University – while plants that include the Parry Pinyon, Parry's Penstemon and Parry's Lily were later named in his honour.

As an accomplished mountaineer, he made barometric measurements of some of Colorado's highest peaks – including the 13,391ft. Parry Peak, so named in his honour following his death in 1890.

In contemporary times, **Bruce Parry** is the British former Royal Marine commando, explorer, trek leader, documentary filmmaker and author born in 1969 in Hythe, Hampshire.

An advocate for the rights of indigenous peoples, integrating himself with them on his expeditions, documentaries he has made include the BBC2 series *Tribe*, began in 2004, and which involved him travelling to far-flung places that include Ethiopia, Indonesia, Mongolia, Siberia and Malaysia.

Leader of an expedition across Greenland to retrace Captain Robert Falcon Scott's ill-fated expedition to the South Pole for the 2006 *Blizzard: Race to the Pole*, he also journeyed through Brazil and Peru for the 2008 series *Amazon*.

Having also led a Children's BBC expedition in 2002 to Borneo to work with orangutans for the series *Serious Jungle*, his many awards include a Royal Television Society Award for Best Children's Factual and Royal Television Society Awards for Best Presenter for both *Tribe* and *Amazon*.